D0116862

ANIMAL ASANAS

YOGA FOR CHILDREN

Leila Kadri Oostendorp

With illustrations by
Elsa Mroziewicz Bahia

PRESTEL

Munich · London · New York

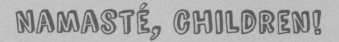

NAMASTÉ, CHILDREN!

NAMASTÉ is our way of saying both hello and goodbye. You do this by simply placing your palms together in front of your chest and bringing them to your forehead with your head bent slightly forward.

Namasté means: The divine in me greets the divine in you.

Whenever we greet each other, be grateful for everything you are and have.

IT'S GREAT THAT YOU HAVE DECIDED TO TAKE UP YOGA!

Yoga is a fun way to stay fit! In yoga it's not important that everything is perfect. Practice as much as you like, so long as you are enjoying it. With more practice, you will find that even the tougher *asanas* (body positions) become easier over time. If you feel any pain when doing the movements, it is important that you stop immediately. Practicing yoga is above all about paying attention to *you*—so that you can learn to work with yourself in order to love all that you are.

This book will show you some amazing exercises. First, take some time to look at the drawings and then carefully and slowly follow the directions. This way you will notice that you feel safe and secure in each position. Be sure to follow the directions for both sides of your body and above all: always breathe in and out through your nose!

Be aware of your breathing as often as possible, especially when you are tired or stressed out. Gently, evenly, and slowly breathe in and out through your nose. Breathing this way during your yoga positions will help relax and calm you.

After a while, you will see how much better, more balanced, and more at ease you are feeling.

Yoga is a gift to yourself! Enjoy every moment of your practice!
I wish you great fun practicing these exercises!

Love, Leila

वृक्षासन
Vrikshasana

THE TREE

THE TREE MEDITATION

Imagine you are a tree. A strong and sturdy tree. Let your roots grow down from your feet deep into the ground—very deep into the earth. Your strong branches stretch out toward the sun and are thick with leaves. You stand firmly on the ground and nobody can move you!

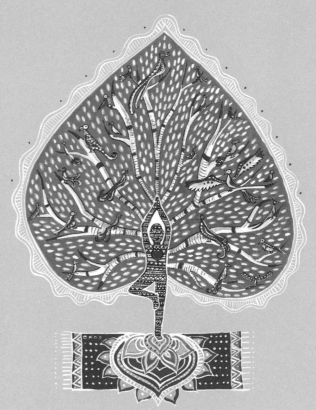

BENEFITS: *Strengthens back muscles, legs, and feet. Corrects posture. Promotes sense of balance, concentration, and confidence. Cultivating stability and evenness develops a safe and harmonious feeling.*

AND HERE'S HOW YOU DO IT!

1 Stand straight with our arms relaxing at the side of your body, your weight balanced evenly on both feet. Your legs are shoulder-width apart. Pay attention to the muscles in your stomach and back. Breathe in deeply through your nose and then slowly out through your nose again. You are in MOUNTAIN POSE (TADASANA)!

2 Shift your weight onto your left leg and relax your right leg. Lift your right knee and rest the sole of the right foot on your left leg. Depending on whether your foot is on your thigh, calf, or ankle—avoid placing your foot on your knee—you can become a big, medium, or small tree.

3 Once you are standing steadily on your left leg, let the branches and leaves of your arms reach out to the sky above and bring the palms of your hands together over your head. Continue breathing slowly and softly through your nose and bask in the warmth of the sun's rays!

4 Remain in this pose for as long as you can and want to. Then repeat the same steps on your right leg.

5 To finish, return to MOUNTAIN POSE and notice how your legs feel. You are nice and warm!

TIP: *Focus your eye on to a single point straight ahead of you. This will help you keep your balance.*

मंडूकासन
Mandukasana

The Frog

BREATHING like a funny **FROG** is something you can do anytime: if you are tired, it gives you energy for the whole day. And when you feel restless, it can really help you relax.

BENEFITS: *This is an asana for both active and tired children. Moving the body in combination with breathing exercises is as relaxing as it is energizing. Activating the breath gives children the energy they need for the challenges of the day. The frog pose is particularly recommended for very active children because it calms their energy and opens them up to relaxation techniques.*

The upper and lower thighs, feet, ankles, and wrists are strengthened. Hips become more flexible.

AND HERE'S HOW YOU DO IT!

1 Stand strong like a MOUNTAIN (TADASANA). Feel your breath move in and out through your whole body.

2 As you breathe in, raise both arms above your head.

3 As you breathe out, fold your upper body over your legs and let your arms and head hang toward the floor.

4 As you breathe in, gently bend your knees and rest your hands on the floor.

5 As you breathe out, lower yourself into a crouch and spread your fingers out on the floor between your legs, raise your head and look straight forward. Imagine you are a vibrant, green frog!

6 As you breathe in again, tighten up your legs and feet. Then, as you breathe out, jump up with your arms stretched out and say, "Ribbit!"

7 Breathe in as you return to a crouch, fingers spread out on the floor between your legs again, and then breathe out again slowly.

8 Keep breathing in and out, getting ready for your next jump—and away you go! **Ribbit!**

9 When you're ready to finish, return to **MOUNTAIN POSE** and place the palms of your hands together a few inches in front of your body. **NAMASTÉ.** Notice your breath moving in and out through the nose. You can achieve anything in life!

TIPS FOR PARENTS WITH LIVELY KIDS: *A relaxing, soft massage in the evening before bedtime can work wonders! Children love back, head, feet, and hand massages. Lively kids are very susceptible to colors. Gentle pastels, such as light blues, greens, yellows, and oranges can sooth the nervous system. Dark shades like grey, black, and brown should be avoided.*

चक्रवाकासन
Chakravakasana

Cat and Cow

Meow! Mooo! This is where you can be as loud as you like!

CAT and COW will energize your tired back. This can help when you first get up in the morning or after a long day at school, and it will straighten your spine. That way you can breathe more easily and feel invigorated.

BENEFITS: *Cat and Cow are ideally done one after the other. Both asanas playfully strengthen and stretch the spine. The back is made stronger and flexible. This wakes up the whole body.*

AND HERE'S HOW YOU DO IT!

1 Begin ON ALL FOURS like a CAT: The palms of your hands and your knees are on the floor, the outspread paws (hands) are under the shoulders and your knees are under the hips. Your spine is straight, your toes are pointing behind you, and your gaze is on the floor. Imagine you are a cute little cat and quite relaxed.

2 As you breathe out, round your back like a cat. At the same time, let your head sink between your arms, moving your chin toward your chest, and point your tail (bottom) down toward the floor, gently pulling your belly in to your navel.

3 Breath in and out deeply and slowly and return to a straight, relaxed back.

4 Now it is the COW'S turn! Breathing in, gently lower your belly toward the floor and at the same time lift your head into the scruff of your neck and your tail (bottom) toward the sky. The front of the neck and your belly are stretched. Now you look like a cheerful cow standing on all fours!

5 Breath out deeply and slowly and return again to a straight, relaxed back.

6 Repeat the asanas for as long as you enjoy it. When you are ready to finish, slowly breathe out and go into CHILD'S POSE (BALASANA): To do this, sit on your heels and lower your upper body toward the floor. At the same time (try to) rest your forehead on the floor without lifting your bottom from your feet. Your big toes are touching and your heels are separated. Your arms are reaching back alongside your body with the palms facing up. Allow your breath to flow evenly and your body to rest.

अधोमुखश्वानासन

Adho Mukha Svanasana

THE DOG

The DOG is man's best friend and that is particularly true for children! There is nothing nicer than going for a walk in the fresh air with your dog or cuddling at home with your loyal companion. It is a lot of fun to do yoga as a dog.

You can wag your tail for sheer joy,
or raise your leg and pee!

BENEFITS: *Calming and energizing. Strengthens the legs, arms, stomach, ankles, and wrists. And it always makes kids laugh.*

AND HERE'S HOW YOU DO IT!

 **Begin** ON ALL FOURS.

As you breathe out, raise your tail (bottom) toward the sky by straightening your legs and say to yourself: I am as friendly as a dog! Your arms and legs should be fully extended. Slowly release your heels to the floor and extend your head between your arms in line with your spine. Each time you breathe out, let your spine sink closer toward the floor. Spread your fingers wide so that there is no space left for fear to hide between your hands and the floor. Once you feel firmly connected to the floor you can practice confidently and comfortably. This is the dog!

DOG TAKING A PEE
(EKA PADA ADHO MUKHA SVANASANA)

 All dogs mark their territory! Every now and then, take turns raising your right leg and your left leg to go "wee-wee". Psssss!

 Finish by returning to ALL FOURS and then going into CHILD'S POSE Notice how good you feel about yourself!

AND YOU CAN DO THIS AS WELL:

Shake your bottom about just like a dog wagging its tail when it is happy.

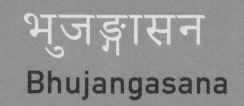

भुजङ्गासन

Bhujangasana

THE COBRA

Anyone who has carefully watched a COBRA will understand why this snake is a symbol of power, bravery, and dignity in India. Cobras are secretive animals. Their skin allows them to be at one with their surroundings and they use their tongue to recognize and catch prey by their scent.

The cobra will improve your concentration and energy levels, reduce your fears, and give you courage and strength.

BENEFITS: *Revitalizing. Strengthens the stomach and the spinal column. Stretches the front of the torso. Deepens the breath. Improves digestion. Inspires self-confidence and clarity.*

AND HERE'S HOW YOU DO IT!

1 Lie down flat on your belly. Your legs are spread slightly apart and your toes are pointing backward. Place your palms on the floor next to your chest with your elbows close to your body. Your forehead is lying gently on the floor and your neck is relaxed. Breathe in and out slowly through your nose. Just imagine you are as focused as a cobra!

2 As you breathe in, press your legs and pelvis down on the floor and slowly raise your upper body.

3 As you breathe out, lift your upper body a tiny bit more by straightening your arms. At the same time, relax your shoulders. Feel how your body is slowly stretching. Your head is straight. Stick out your tongue like a cobra and hisss! You are brave!

4 On your next out-breath, bend your arms again and then push yourself back into CHILD'S POSE.

YOU CAN ALSO TRY THIS:

The TWISTING COBRA (TRIYAK BHUJANGASANA): When breathing out in the cobra position, twist your upper body and head to the left and then look over your left shoulder toward your left heel (or if you want to twist deeper, look at your right heel). Breathe in and then slowly move forward. Breathe out and twist to the other side.

TIP: *Whenever your back is a little stiff, go into the* SNAKE POSE *by gently raising your upper body and hands from the floor.*

एकपाद कपोतासन

Eka Pada Kapotasana

THE DOVE

DOVES are intelligent and versatile birds that adapt well to their surroundings. In earlier days, people found use for them as carrier pigeons. Nowadays, doves are seen as a symbol of peace and hope.

BENEFITS: *Good workout for strengthening back muscles. Excellent stretch for the bottom, stomach, hips, and shoulder muscles.*

This asana opens up your heart and develops mental flexibility. This is an ideal exercise to help you wind down after a busy day as it relieves tension and helps you get back to feeling yourself.

AND HERE'S HOW YOU DO IT!

1 Go ON ALL FOURS like a cat: your hands are spread out on the floor beneath your shoulders, your knees beneath your hips. Your back should be straight and relaxed, your toes pointing behind you, and your gaze is on the floor.

2 Now breathe out and extend your left leg along the floor behind you. This is going to become the tail of the dove. Breathe in and rest your bottom on to your right ankle. Your claws (fingers) are now firmly placed on the floor in front of your front knee. Your back is still straight, your toes are pointing backward, and you are looking straight ahead.

3 Take a breath in and bend your upper body gently back (keep your lower body pressing forward). Stretch your chest outward and fill it with energy and fresh air. Your neck, stomach, and arms are stretched and your shoulders are relaxed.

4 When you breathe out again, lower your upper body toward the floor, stretching your arms out in front of you and gently resting your forehead on the floor. Gently breath in and out and feel how your body relaxes.

5 Take in some deep, long breaths and get back ON ALL FOURS. Now it is your other leg's turn! When you're done, rest on your heels, place your forehead on the floor and stretch out your arms. Notice how happy and proud you feel!

बद्धकोणासन
Baddha Konasana

THE BUTTERFLY

Just imagine you are a cheerful and colorful BUTTERFLY,
perhaps a red admiral or a blue mountain swallowtail.
Your legs are its big wings and your hands are its long
antennae.

What color butterfly are you?
Maybe your favorite color?

BENEFITS: *Fights fatigue. Helps to keep the hip joints and inner and upper
thighs flexible. A good workout for the spine.*

AND HERE'S HOW YOU DO IT!

1 Sit on the floor with your legs straight in front of
you, your hands on the floor next to your hips.
This is the STAFF POSE (DANDASANA).

2  Bring one knee into the chest and then carefully lower it to side, then do the same with the other knee.

3  Touch the soles of the feet together and close your hands around them. Now slowly move your wings (knees) up and down like a fluttering butterfly—softly and gently.

You are now flying freely and briskly above a pretty meadow. You see flowers of every color. This inspires you to fly farther and farther. You feel alive and happy! You can smell the fragrance of the flowers. One sweet smell after another making you more and more relaxed.

4 After a long flight, you are now back on your mat. Release your feet and relax your arms. To finish, slowly straighten one leg after the other and gently bounce them on the floor.

YOU CAN ALSO TRY THIS:

Using your antennae you can see better when you are flying. To do this pose you have to be strong in order to hold your back straight. Bring the backs of both hands up to your forehead and point both index fingers upward. Your fingers are now sticking out just like butterfly antennae. Now you can fly off into the wide world with ease.

TIP: *If it becomes too hard to keep your back straight, you can always first try to lean your back against a wall to support you.*

उष्ट्रासन
Ustrasana

The Camel

The **CAMEL** is an animal with extraordinary talents. Sturdy and durable, it can go without water for over a week. You can train yourself to be as steadfast as a camel especially when you face difficult challenges. This is not an easy exercise. It requires lots of energy and concentration.

Stay focused, you can do it!

BENEFITS: *Develops good posture, strengthens muscles around the stomach, pelvis, upper thighs, and back. Deepens the breath and exercises the diaphragm. Stimulates the digestive system and calms the nervous system.*

Kids with lots of energy absolutely love this asana. Small children may not have the strength to hold this pose for long, but they will be eager to practice it. It also takes a lot of concentration and balance. Children should be encouraged when they face these challenges. Ustrasana will boost self-awareness and self-confidence.

AND HERE'S HOW YOU DO IT!

1 Rest on your heels. Your spine is upright, your ribs are moving forward, and your shoulders are relaxed. Rest your hands on your thighs and gently breathe in and out. Try to enjoy this pose. This is the KNEELING POSITION (VAJRASANA).

2 As you breathe in, rise up onto your knees and bring your legs hip-width apart, the tops of your feet are on the floor and your toes pointing back. Look straight ahead with your arms relaxed and at your sides. Take deep, soft breaths in and out and imagine you are a strong camel roaming the desert!

3 Breathing in, keep the tops of your toes on the floor or tuck them so your heels are higher. At the same time, your right arm begins to move forward and encircles your head. Your gaze follows your hand.

4 Your arm continues to move in a big circle backward until your hand grasps your right ankle or your heel. At the same time, move your pelvis as far forward as possible so you're your back creates a stable arch. Your gaze is still to the front.

5 Breathe in and repeat the same with the left arm until both hands are at your feet. Be mindful of keeping your eyes open. Breathe in and out and be aware of your breathing, feel the position.

6 When you are finished, rest on your ankles and bend forward into CHILD'S POSE. Relax and say to yourself: "I am happy."

कूर्मासन
Kurmasana

The Tortoise

TORTOISES are survivors from prehistoric times. They are very clever and know exactly when it is time to pull back and take a break. After millions of years on this earth, they have learned to keep calm—after all, they have all the time in the world.

People can learn a lot from tortoises, especially about doing things at the right time and with calmness.

BENEFITS: *Stretches and stimulates the spine. Stimulates the inner organs. Brings peace, a sense of wellbeing, serenity.*

AND HERE'S HOW YOU DO IT!

1 Sit on your bottom with your legs straight out in front of you, your torso upright, and the palms of your hands flat on the floor next to your hips (DANDASANA).

2 Breathing out bend both knees into the body and let them open out to the sides, pressing the soles of your feet together. Hold your feet in your hands and lean forward from the hips, just as we did in the butterfly pose.

3 On your next out-breath, release your feet and slide both arms under your knees so that your palms are on the floor outside your feet.

Imagine that both arms are two earthworms. The earthworms are slithering through the holes, curving back on themselves, and meeting each other at the front. One says to the other: Hey! What are you up to? I am practicing yoga, what about you? Me, too! Then let's do yoga together and they both embrace.

Wiggle your bottom a bit to the right then to the left to make sure you are sitting securely on the floor. As you breathe in slowly stretch your head forward as if you are sniffing at a wonderfully fragrant flower.

4 It's time to take a break by pulling your head back into your shell. As you breathe out let your head release downward so that your forehead rests on the floor. Take care to keep your back straight. You feel safe and sound in your shell! Close your eyes and enjoy the calm.

5 Breathe in and slowly raise your head and upper body. Stretch your legs out again and rest your hands on your thighs.

6 Breathing out, pull your knees in toward your chest, wrap your arms around them, and make yourself small and round. Breathe in and gently roll onto your back. Rock back and forth just like a tortoise on its shell. Enjoy this nice back massage!

7 Finish off by lying flat on your back with your arms alongside your body. You feel comfortable and secure just like a tortoise!

YOU CAN ALSO TRY THIS:

Instead of joining the soles of your feet together, keep your feet wide apart, relax the bend in your knees, and lean forward by extending the spine. With the heels on the floor, stretch your arms out wide under your knees and slide them back and forth like a sea turtle. If it feels comfortable, lower your head to the floor.

सिंहगर्जनासन
Simha Garjanasana

The Roaring Lion

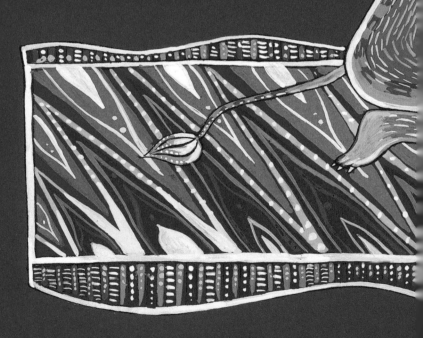

THE LION is the king among all animals!
He slowly, steadily, and serenely prowls through
the African savanna in true feline fashion.
When the lion appears, most animals show great
respect! He's a large, strong, and powerful cat.

As a lion, you can be as loud as you like!
Roar your head and your heart off whenever
you need to let off steam!

BENEFITS: *Boosts self-confidence and develops verbal abilities.*
Eases tension and stress. Helps let off steam. Fills the body and
soul with energy. Helps lively children become more composed.
Eye muscles get a solid workout and are strengthened.

AND HERE'S HOW YOU DO IT!

1 Sit calmly like a lion on your heels. Your paws (hands) are on the floor in front of your knees, your arms are long. Your back is stretched and leaning forward from your hips, your neck is long and your gaze is to the front. You are silent and motionless like a cat.

2 Only your eyes look right and left, up and down. Nothing will escape your notice!

3 Breathe in and while breathing out show that you are the lion king: shake your magnificent mane!

4 Hold your head still and breathe in deeply through your nose. As you breathe out, lift up on your knees and show off your claws by lifting your arms off the floor and spreading your bent fingers wide. Now stick out your tongue as far as possible and roar with as much power as you can. Breathe in again and when breathing out roar mightily again from the bottom of your stomach. Roar as often as you like.

Can you touch your chin when you roar?

5 On breathing in again sit on your heels and resume your CHILD'S POSE as you breathe out. You are strong and mighty!

शशांकासन
Shashankasana

THE RABBIT

RABBITS are special individuals! They adapt to different surroundings, they can live in groups or alone, and they are sweet and cuddly animals. They are born with big, wide-open eyes, meaning they miss nothing from the very start. They have strong legs that allow them to run fast and they have long ears so they can hear everything!

As a rabbit, you point your ears upward. You check everything around you. What noises are there around you? As a rabbit you can hear everything!
You are awake and alert!

BENEFITS: *Promotes a sense of security and safety. Has a soothing effect and boosts concentration. Relaxes the shoulder, neck, and the back. Also good for the heart and deepens breathing.*

AND HERE'S HOW YOU DO IT!

1 Take up the **KNEELING POSITION (VAJRASANA)**. Your spine should be upright, your chest puffed out, your shoulders loose, and your arms resting at your side. Breathe in and then slowly breathe out.

2 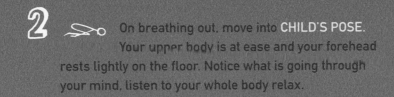 On breathing out, move into CHILD'S POSE. Your upper body is at ease and your forehead rests lightly on the floor. Notice what is going through your mind, listen to your whole body relax.

3 As you breathe in, clasp your fingers behind your back, lift your seat and come onto your knees as you rest the top of your head gently on the floor. Your ears are long and you can hear everything that is going on around you. Stay in that position for as long as you wish.

4 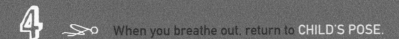 When you breathe out, return to CHILD'S POSE.

5 When you are ready to finish, slowly lift up your upper body and return to the KNEELING POSITION with a nice straight back.

YOU CAN ALSO TRY THIS:

THE STANDING RABBIT: Touch your legs together and bring your back upright. Clasp your fingers behind your back, bend your body slightly forward from the waist and lift your arms up to the sky as far as you can manage.

TIP: *The standing rabbit is particularly good for loosening up your ribcage and shoulder. If you carry a backpack to school every day, this is a good pose for you to try.*

शलभासन
Shalabhasana

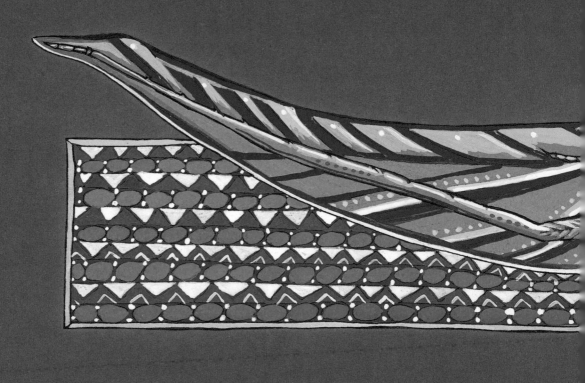

THE LOCUST

THE LOCUST is a lovely exercise, but you need
a lot of strength and concentration to pull this asana off!
Just give it a go!

BENEFITS: *Strengthens the stomach and lower back muscles, as well as
your bottom. Stretches the chest and shoulder muscles. Relaxes organs inside
the belly and helps the digestive system.*

AND HERE'S HOW YOU DO IT!

1 Lie on your belly. Your back is straight,
your legs together, and your head is turned to one side.
Your arms are relaxed next to your body and your palms
are facing up.

2 AIR BALLOON BREATHING:

Just imagine you had a balloon in your belly. When you
breathe in, the balloon gets bigger and so does your
belly; when you breathe out, your belly gets smaller.

Breathe in, your belly is big and breathe out,
your belly gets smaller. Do this three times
and notice how your body feels.

3 When you breathe out, try to make your body as stiff as a board and touch the floor with your chin.

4 As you breathe in, lift your chest, head, and your right leg. Look forward. As you breathe out, everything drops back into place. Switch sides as you breathe in, repeat everything, but this time lift your left leg.

5 Now prepare for the full position. Take a deep breath in and raise your chest, head, legs, and arms from the mat all at the same time. Your legs are extended, your arms are close to your body, and your shoulders are pulling backward. Your whole body is like a drawn bow. You face forward and remain very attentive. Breathe in and out for as long as you feel comfortable.

6 When you breathe out one last time, rest down on the mat with your head turned to one side.

7 Finish off by resuming CHILD'S POSE.

YOU COULD ALSO TRY THIS:

You can try different arm positions.

1. Clasp your fingers behind your back and breathe out, stretching your arms further back like wings just before taking flight.

2. Stretch both arms forwards, like a superman!

मत्स्यासन

Matsyasana

THE FISH

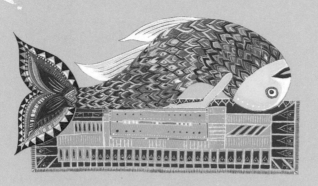

Imagine you are a FISH. Your legs are the tail and your bent elbows are the fins. You are calmly swimming among the coral in warm, blue waters. Your scales are glistening joyfully in marvelously bright colors. You are calm and peaceful.

BENEFITS: *This is an asana better known as the "destroyer of all illnesses." The pose liberates and opens up the ribcage and heart, freeing you of everything that is worrying you. The fish refreshes body and soul, especially after a long day at school, and it also boosts confidence. This is good for weary little champions and helps restore and reset their body, mind, and spirit.*

Improves spine flexibility and strength, as well as posture in the upper back. Stimulates the inner organs, the neck, the heart, circulation, and the respiratory and nervous system. It also helps relieve stress and anxiety.

AND HERE'S HOW YOU DO IT!

1 Lie down flat on your back. Place your legs and feet closely together and point your toes. Your arms are lying comfortably next to your body, your palms facing downward. Breathe gently in and out.

2 Slide your hands under your seat toward your upper thigh, keeping your arms close to your body. As you breathe in, lift your upper back off the floor as you bend your elbows and release the top of your head back onto the floor. Your forearms and palms are pressing down on the floor.

3 When you breathe out, let your head drop backward as far as possible. On breathing in, stretch your ribcage upwards. Relax your backside to avoid your back becoming hollow.

4 Your upper body creates an arch, while the top of your head rests on the floor. Your body weight should be placed on your lower arms and elbows and not on your head. Close your eyes and take note of your breathing for a while.

5 When you breathe out one last time, gently release your upper body to the floor and then lie flat on your back.

6 Draw both knees into the body and wrap your arms around them. Stay in this rolled up position for a few breaths of air.

7 Now relax into the SPAGHETTI POSE (SAVASANA). Lie down on your back like spaghetti pasta just before you cook it. Spread your legs hip-width apart and open your feet slightly outward. Relax your arms next to your body with the palms facing up. Or place your hands on your belly. Open your mouth slightly and soften your tongue. Draw your chin into your chest. You can close your eyes. Notice your breath moving in and out.

53

मकरासन

Makarasana

The Crocodile

Which is the stronger of the two: a CROCODILE or a lion? The crocodile has a huge, frighteningly scary mouth as well as a long and very powerful tail. The crocodile can use its tail to swim and dive fast and to chase big animals in the water or even on the ground. Older crocodiles do not really have any enemies. They also reach a great old age because they have cleverly learned the ancient ways of being able to relax.

This exercise will bring life into your backbone and help you get up in the morning!

BENEFITS: *Helps relieve tension in the back and opens up blocked energy. Relaxes the neck and helps unwind weary backs and minds. Stretches the chest muscles, deepens breathing, and stimulates the digestive system.*

AND HERE'S HOW YOU DO IT!

1 Get started in the SPAGHETTI POSE: Lie down on your back, legs slighty open, your feet tilting outward. Place both arms next to your body with the palms facing up.

2 As you breathe out, bring your legs close together and stretch out your arms to the side and on the same level as your shoulders. The palms of your hands are now flat on the floor.

3 Bend your knees and draw your heels in as close to your bottom as possible. Press your knees together hard and let your legs slant toward the floor on the right. This is the crocodile's tail. Turn your head to the left and look at your left hand. Try to rest your shoulders on the floor, broad and flat. Feel how your twist deepens as you breathe in and out. Use this moment for calm relaxation.

Relax your whole body and breathe in and out several times, gently and slowly. Just imagine you are a mighty crocodile lying at the riverbank and taking in the sun's warm rays. The water makes a pleasant noise, which brings you ever increasing tranquility.

4 Listen to your body and then breathing out slowly return to your original position. Switch sides.

5 Repeat this asana a couple of times and then finish off by resting quietly in the SPAGHETTI POSE.

YOU COULD ALSO TRY THIS:

1. Turn on your stomach, extending both arms above your head and place the palms of your hands together. Turn on to one side of your body and open and close your arms like the jaws of a crocodile. Make a big smile at the end!

2. Bend your right knee (keeping the left straight) and slowly roll onto your left side until the right knee touches the floor. Turn your head to the right and then switch sides.

TIP: *Playing the sound of running water is great for this exercise.*

57

RELAXATION EXERCISES

At the end of your yoga exercises, lie flat on your back! Your legs are spread comfortably apart and your feet gently fall open to the sides. Your arms rest peacefully next to your body and the palms of your hands face up. Take regular and gentle breaths, in and out.

JUST RELAX, UNWIND, AND CLOSE YOUR EYES IF YOU WISH.
TAKE YOURSELF ON AN IMAGINARY JOURNEY.

Imagine it is a late springtime afternoon and you have gotten all your homework out of the way. It has just stopped raining and you go outside into the fresh air. You can hear the birds twittering and you notice them busily fluttering from one tree to the other. Up in the sky, you see a bright rainbow.

You sit down on a wooden bench and make yourself comfortable, gazing at the rainbow with its wonderful, vibrant colors that put you at ease. You inhale and exhale the fresh air, you look closely at each color and then say to yourself:

RED: I am fit. I am healthy. I am brave. I am strong.

ORANGE: I am happy. I am creative. I feel good about myself.

YELLOW: I am bright. I am friendly. I am full of confidence. Just feel how the color yellow gives you warmth and fills you with joy and happiness.

GREEN: I am calm and balanced. I am connected harmoniously to nature. I am full of life.

BLUE: I am relaxed. I am focused. I am in harmony with myself and my friends. I am reliable.

INDIGO: I feel light and free. I can feel the light within me. I know who I am.

VIOLET: I am confident and friendly. I have fun with my friends. I am open to all things that come my way.

You are enjoying the moment and hear the birds singing. You look down at your feet and discover the first flowers of the season coming up from the ground. You can smell the light scents of spring all around you. The wet soil, damp grass, the flowers, the trees, and the leaves. You take one deep breath, stand up, and slowly head home.

A wonderful day draws to an end.

NAMASTÉ, PARENTS!

Childhood is an intensive period of physical, emotional, social, and spiritual growth.

It's a time characterized by a great desire to be up and about and to discover things with insatiable curiosity. Yoga can complement and support your kids' development in the deepest ways imaginable.

Yoga can help children manage the busy schedules they often have today. The conscious practice of connecting movement with breath helps children cultivate both a healthy body image and a calm, safe space inside themselves where they can recharge their batteries and let go of stress.

Yoga's holistic approach—with its physical exercises (Asanas) that are often derived from the worlds of animals and plants, its breathing techniques (Pranayama), as well as its concentration, awareness, and relaxation exercises—can encourage children to choose to lead a healthy and balanced life from an early stage in their development.

This harmonizing effect of yoga on children has been championed by a number of scientific studies. Yoga stimulates all senses, improves perception, and helps foster a healthy sense of self-confidence in children. What's more, yoga improves concentration and performance levels.

This book will allow you to explore the dynamic, fun, and fulfilling world of yoga together with your children. These easy-to-understand yoga exercises will help your kids stay vibrant and focused throughout the week while they're at school, relax on the weekend or whenever they need to. It is important to note that time spent doing these yoga exercises is for the children's enjoyment and exploration; it is not a time to be achievement-oriented or critical.

And don't hold yourself back from practicing too! All of the exercises in this book are not only suitable for kids, but also for older children and grown-ups!

I hope you and your kids have a lot of fun!

Yours,
Leila Kadri Oostendorp

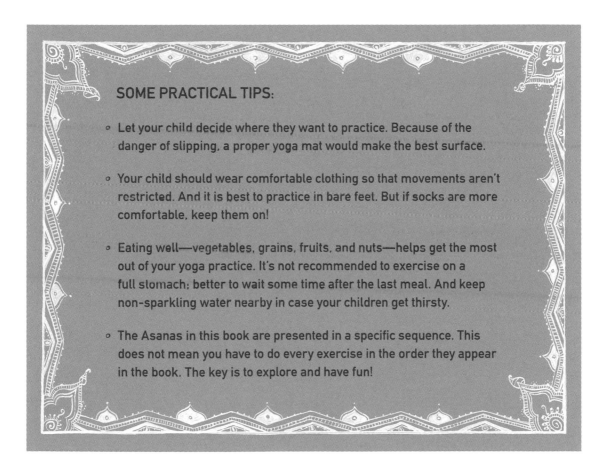

SOME PRACTICAL TIPS:

◦ Let your child decide where they want to practice. Because of the danger of slipping, a proper yoga mat would make the best surface.

◦ Your child should wear comfortable clothing so that movements aren't restricted. And it is best to practice in bare feet. But if socks are more comfortable, keep them on!

◦ Eating well—vegetables, grains, fruits, and nuts—helps get the most out of your yoga practice. It's not recommended to exercise on a full stomach; better to wait some time after the last meal. And keep non-sparkling water nearby in case your children get thirsty.

◦ The Asanas in this book are presented in a specific sequence. This does not mean you have to do every exercise in the order they appear in the book. The key is to explore and have fun!

CONTENT

Here is a listing of all the exercises described in this book. The page number refers to the page where you find the instruction for the particular exercise.

THE AUTHOR

A native Brazilian, LEILA KADRI OOSTENDORP lives with her two children in Munich. She is considered one of the most respected teachers of yoga for children and young people. Her many years of experience in this field come to life in her training and advanced instruction courses for teachers of yoga for kids, as well as in her workshops for educators and teachers alike. Leila provides her courses in German, English, Portuguese, and Spanish.

Her yoga classes are warm, creative, dynamic, sensitive, and above all supportive in the personal development and self-awareness of all participants. Leila's enthusiasm inspires a lifelong love of yoga in both children and parents. It is her heartfelt mission to bring yoga to children all over the world. For more info, please visit: www.kinderyogawelt.de.

SAFETY NOTE:

The information, practices, and poses in this book are not offered as medical advice or suggested as treatment for any condition that might require medical attention. To avoid injury, practice yoga with a skilled instructor and consult a health professional to determine your body's needs and limitations. The writer and publisher hereby disclaim any liability from injuries resulting from following any recommendation in this book.

A special note of thanks to Leila's yoga teacher from India, Prasad Ragnekar, for his thorough and diligent assistance with the Sanskrit translations.

© 2017, Prestel Verlag, Munich · London · New York
A member of Verlagsgruppe Random House GmbH
Neumarkter Strasse 28 · 81673 Munich

Prestel Publishing Ltd.
14-17 Wells Street
London, W1T 3PD

Prestel Publishing
900 Broadway, Suite 603
New York, NY 10003

Library of Congress Control Number: 2016954055
A CIP catalogue record for this book is available from the British Library.

Editorial direction: Doris Kutschbach
Translated from the German: Paul Kelly
Copyediting: John Son
Design and layout: Meike Sellier
Production management: Astrid Wedemeyer, Lisa Preissler
Separations: Reproline Mediateam, Munich
Printing and binding: DZS, d.o.o., Ljublijana
Paper: Offset

Verlagsgruppe Random House FSC®N001967
Printed in Bosnia

ISBN 978-3-7913-7275–4
www.prestel.com